LIBRARIES NI
WITHDRAWN FROM STOCK

D0363389

Elephant Rescue

A True Story

Written by
Louisa Leaman

Orion
Children's Books

ORION CHILDREN'S BOOKS

First published in Great Britain in 2015 by Orion Children's Books
This edition published in Great Britain in 2016 by Hodder and Stoughton

1 3 5 7 9 10 8 6 4 2

Copyright © Hachette Children's Group, 2015
Text copyright © Louisa Leaman, 2015
Louisa Leaman has asserted her right to be identified as the author of this work.
Images copyright © Born Free Foundation Limited

By arrangement with Born Free Foundation Ltd
The Born Free Foundation logo is a trademark of the Born Free Foundation
Ltd and used under license
Born Free Foundation logo copyright © Born Free Foundation 2001

All rights reserved.
No part of this publication may be reproduced, stored in
a retrieval system, or transmitted, in any form or by any means, without
the prior permission in writing of the publisher, nor be otherwise circulated
in any form of binding or cover other than that in which it is published
and without a similar condition including this condition being
imposed on the subsequent purchaser.

A CIP catalogue record for this book is available from the British Library.

ISBN 978 1 5101 0133 3

Printed and bound in China

The paper and board used in this book are from
well-managed forestsand other responsible sources.

Orion Children's Books
An imprint of
Hachette Children's Group
Part of Hodder and Stoughton
Carmelite House
50 Victoria Embankment
London EC4Y 0DZ

An Hachette UK Company
www.hachette.co.uk

www.hachettechildrens.co.uk

Photo copyright ©Maria Slough

Hello everyone,

I expect that when people read the words The Born Free Foundation they think of lions. And that is right, as it was the story of Elsa the lioness in Joy Adamson's book '*Born Free*' that encouraged us all to think about lions and how they live. Not only that of course, but what they need to live fulfilled and natural lives.

At Born Free we have, over many years, been able to give some lions who suffered in miserable and unnatural conditions in captivity, a second chance in our African rescue centres. But this book is not about lions. We now help all kinds of different animals and these stories are about two very special elephants. Nina is an African elephant and Pinkie lives in Sri Lanka. They belong in different countries but they share the same needs. Elephants are caring, family, social animals. They protect their young and they mourn their old when they die. In fact, they are quite like human beings. And, like human beings, if a little elephant loses its mother, it will not survive unless someone rescues it and cares for it.

The stories of Nina and Pinkie are different as you will read, but they have several things in common. The first is that elephant orphans need help from us – and this they both received, thanks to Born Free, to Tony Fitzjohn in Tanzania, and our Patron Martin Clunes who gave his support and blessing to Nina's rehabilitation. And in far-off Sri Lanka, Pinkie was nurtured and cared for by Dr Suhada and the team at the Elephant Transit Home. Our wonderful Patron

Helen Worth paid a visit for us to the Transit Home, and was thrilled to be able to give Pinkie her milk feed.

We all rejoice when wild animals can live free, as nature intended. In these two stories you will see that for Nina and Pinkie, in different ways, this has been possible. And the understanding and kindness of all the people who helped them is something I shall always be grateful for.

Virginia McKenna
Actress and Founder Trustee, Born Free Foundation

BORN FREE AROUND THE WORLD

Animal Welfare

Born Free exposes animal suffering and fights cruelty.

Wild Animal Rescue

Born Free develops and supports many wild animal rescue centres.

Canada

United Kingdom

USA

South America

Conservation

Born Free protects wild animals in their natural habitat.

Communities and Education

Born Free works closely with communities who live alongside the projects we support.

Europe

China

India

Vietnam

Africa

Indonesia

This is the real-life story of how two elephants from different continents were given the gift of freedom, thanks to the effort and care provided by Born Free and many others. Nina, an orphaned African elephant, lived for 27 years in captivity before being returned to the wild.

Pinkie, a baby Asian elephant, suffered terrible injuries before finding confidence at an elephant orphanage.

Moving an elephant from one location to another is a massive challenge. Nina and Pinkie's stories are full of danger, drama, tragedy, triumph – and a few surprises!

Nina

FACTFILE

- Born in the wild in Tanzania

- Orphaned when she was six months old

- Favourite treats – bananas and cake

- Personality – very gentle and friendly, but nervous of new experiences

- Became a TV star when she was filmed by the BBC

Pinkie

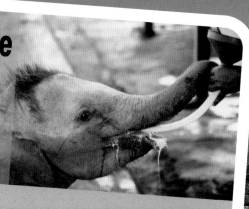

FACTFILE

- Born in the wild in Sri Lanka

- Named Pinkie because of the long pink scar on her face

- Food – as a baby she was fed a special milk formula through a funnel

- Favourite activity – looking after other elephants in her herd

- Personality – confident and caring

Learn a new elephant fact
every time you see me.

Nina's Story
Chapter One

Tanzania

Beneath a fierce sun, above the red earth of the Tanzanian plain, a pair of vultures circled over a baby elephant. For several hours, she had been huddling beside a thorn bush, not far from a muddy watering hole.

Where she'd come from and why she was alone at the watering hole was a mystery. She was no more than six months old, so she should have been with her mother.

Usually only adult males – the bulls – can be seen

wandering on their own. Females, along with their young and old, stick together in a close-knit family group and are led by a dominant older female known as the 'matriarch'. When families get together they form herds that can number hundreds of individual elephants.

This lonely elephant calf was too young to feed herself. Her trunk was only just beginning to get the muscle strength and control required to help it find food and suck up water. She was also vulnerable to all the dangers of the wild including predators such as lions and hyenas.

Elephants rely on suckling milk from their mothers until they are two or three years old. When a new calf is born, the whole family rejoices. They all love the calf and play a part in keeping it safe. The matriarch, usually the oldest of the adult females, shares her knowledge with the rest of the herd, helping them find food and leading them to watering holes.

For the little elephant in this real-life story, however, her family had gone. While we'll never know for certain what happened to her mother – possibly she had fallen victim to poachers illegally hunting and killing elephants for their ivory tusks – she was alone and confused and longing for the gentle caress of her mother's trunk.

Because of ivory's high price, the illegal ivory trade continues even though it involves great cruelty. Thousands of elephants are killed and their tusks – symbols of their strength and splendour – are viciously hacked off. The body of the elephant is left to stain the African soil, while the ivory is smuggled to far corners of the world, to make jewellery and ornaments.

With no mother, no family, the vultures circling and the sun starting to set, another dark, frightening and possibly fatal night lay in wait for this baby.

As if things couldn't get any worse for the calf, she heard a rumbling in the ground. She felt it through her padded feet, vibrating up through her legs. She lifted her head and flapped her ears in alarm. She saw two dazzling lights attached to a fast-moving thing that she had never seen before.

She waited and watched.

Nina's Story
Chapter Two

Mount Meru

The 'thing' coming towards her was a Land Rover. A man stepped out of it and came towards the elephant calf. Thankfully, this particular man was no poacher. He was called Bandi Schwendt Nagy and he liked wildlife. Bandi ran a small private zoo in northern Tanzania called the Mount Meru Wildlife Sanctuary. When he spotted the elephant calf on her own, he knew she would never survive. What's more, he thought she would be a very interesting animal to have in his zoo. There were probably no other captive elephants in Tanzania. She'd be a talking point.

He took her back with him in his Land Rover.

Mount Meru Wildlife Sanctuary, just outside Arusha, was nestled in the foothills of Mount Meru, not far from the mighty Mount Kilimanjaro, Africa's highest mountain, on the banks of the Usa River. It welcomed tourists who wanted to see African wildlife, such as ostrich, waterbuck, zebra and buffalo,

as well as an enormous variety of exotic birds.

Bandi and his team always had good intentions for the little elephant calf. They named her 'Nina'. They made sure she had food and drink and protection. But unfortunately, the zoo was small and her enclosure was tiny. This made Nina unhappy.

FACT FILE

An animal as large as an elephant needs room to roam and feed. They need wide open spaces over which to roam and to forage for food. Their days are spent eating, drinking, wandering, bathing, dusting, wallowing, playing and resting.

Above all, elephants need the company of other elephants. Remember, female elephants never live on their own. They live their entire lives surrounded by their friends and relations.

As Nina grew in size, the Mount Meru enclosure began to feel very cramped indeed. It was here, within these boundaries, that she spent the next 27 years of her life – 27 years in the same tiny space, alone.

Day after day, Nina desperately anticipated the brief moments of human contact when her keepers would come to feed her, guests would come to admire her or Bandi would drop by to say hello. She had a very gentle nature and never showed aggression. Although she was lonely, she was very accepting of the humans surrounding her. They were all she knew. She had only briefly experienced life as part of an elephant family when she would have followed her mother, aunts, sisters and brothers down to the nearest watering hole, to bathe, drink and play under the curious gaze of a flock of egrets or a raft of hippo. In the zoo she only saw people and walls and concrete and bales of dry straw.

FACT FILE

Elephants are highly sociable animals. They like company and they travel together. They are regularly seen interlocking their trunks to 'hug' each other and have special greeting ceremonies for friends. They experience a range of emotions much like people – joy, sorrow and anger. It is even thought that they 'mourn' the loss of loved ones. They have been known to gently touch the skulls and tusks of the dead with their trunks and feet.

It became obvious to Bandi that Nina was lonely and frustrated. She started swaying her head repetitively, which wasn't typical elephant behaviour. This head-swaying was her attempt to stimulate herself, to find something to fill the space that in the wild she would have filled with interesting activities, such as foraging for food, digging for water, stripping the tasty bark off tree branches and socialising with members of her elephant family and the wider herd.

Many elephants, when kept in captivity, adopt repetitive behaviours. They pace or rock or shake their heads. Some people say they go mad.

Eventually, Bandi began to wonder whether the only way to improve Nina's quality of life was to give her the chance to return to the wild. However, 27 years was a very long time to be in captivity. Such a drastic change of lifestyle might be impossible for Nina – but as Bandi stared into her sad eyes, with their long, pretty eyelashes, he realised he had to at least give her the chance.

Nina's Story
Chapter Three

Born Free to the Rescue

In 1997, Bandi contacted Will Travers who ran the Born Free Foundation, to see if they might be able to help. He asked Will if Born Free could provide a more suitable home for Nina, where she could meet other elephants and enjoy a natural life.

Born Free, one of the UK's leading wildlife charities, was excited about the challenge, but had lots of concerns.

Firstly, there was the matter of getting the right team together – releasing an elephant, especially one that has been so long in captivity, is a difficult task. If they were going to make a success of it, they had to find the right people with the right expertise.

FACT FILE

Although elephants look sturdy, they can be surprisingly delicate. It is dangerous for an elephant to lie down for long periods of time, because the weight of one lung can crush the other, restrict breathing and lead to suffocation and death.

It was decided that Nina's safety should be the number one priority throughout the project. Born Free contacted a Zimbabwean elephant translocation expert called Clem Coetzee, who agreed to fly to Tanzania to supervise the move. As well as Clem, many other helpers were asked to get involved, including vets, wildlife experts, park rangers and officials. The Born Free Foundation worked day and night to raise the money needed to pay all the costs, and to make sure all the necessary permits and paperwork were in place.

The next thing they needed to do was to find a

suitable vehicle. Luckily, Born Free were able to
enlist the help of the Kenya Wildlife Service's unique

elephant relocation truck, Hannibal, which they'd donated to Kenya several years before. Hannibal was purpose-built, with huge wheels, a powerful engine, the strength to support the weight of a large elephant

and a special crate to carry an elephant in.

Then, of course, they had to find a safe place where Nina could be returned to a wild and free life. Will contacted one of his good friends, Tony Fitzjohn, a

wildlife expert, living and working as Field Director of the George Adamson Wildlife Preservation Trust in Tanzania. Tony had, for many years, been the right-hand man of George Adamson, the famous conservationist, who together with his wife Joy had returned Elsa the lioness to the wild. Will asked if he could offer a future to Nina at the remote and enormous Mkomazi National Reserve where he lived, about 250 kilometres from Bandi's zoo.

Thankfully, Tony agreed.

Years before, Tony had been granted permission by the Tanzanian Government to set up his camp in the 2,000 square kilometre Mkomazi National Reserve.

He'd built roads through the red dust and cut aircraft landing strips into the thick, thorny bush. Since Mkomazi is such a dry area he also had to make sure there were enough water sources for animals and humans. He'd then employed and trained a team of local rangers.

Although Tony had already a rhino sanctuary and centre for the highly endangered African Wild Dog, he'd never worked with elephants before and knew little about them. The first thing to do was to build a special temporary compound for Nina where she could get used to her new surroundings. The compound, called a 'boma', would be a place for Nina to adjust before being fully released into the wild.

As preparations started to take shape, one question

continued to worry Will, Clem and Tony: after 27 years in captivity would Nina cope with life outside of Mount Meru Wildlife Sanctuary ? Would she know how to get food and water? Would she be accepted by the local elephants? And would the open space amaze or terrify her?

Nina had only had a short time living with her herd before being orphaned and taken in by Bandi. It was difficult to know what she would remember and whether she'd still have the instincts of a free, wild elephant.

There is a well-known saying: an elephant never forgets. Elephants' memories are, indeed, remarkable. In fact, an elephant's memory is an important survival tool. For example, during the dry season, a matriarch might need to guide her family, sometimes for tens of miles, to a watering hole she remembers from years ago. Her good memory helps her increase her family's chances of survival.

Nina's amazing journey was such an incredible story that Born Free and the BBC agreed to make a film about it for their popular 'Born to be Wild' TV series. Of course, the chance of telling Nina's story

to the world was a wonderful opportunity but it did create extra complications. In addition to Nina the elephant, they now had to work with a large TV crew and all their cameras and equipment. But Will and the Born Free team had a hunch that the effort would be worth it. They were sure that allowing millions of people to share in Nina's great adventure, with all its ups and downs, would touch hearts around the world and make people think twice about whether animals like elephants should be locked up in captivity for life in zoos and circuses.

The presenter of the 'Born to be Wild' programme was a famous English actor called Martin Clunes. Martin loved elephants and was delighted to be involved. As the team began to arrive at Mount Meru, Martin spent as much time as he could with Nina and Bandi, getting to know her, hoping she would trust him – a string of ripe bananas helped. Martin fell in love.

An anxious excitement crackled in the air. Nina's big day – the first of many – was just around the corner.

Nina, meanwhile, observed preparations from her enclosure. She probably wondered what all the fuss was about. Certainly she enjoyed the extra attention and 'treats' and the company of her new friend, Martin. Looking out across the open space beyond the fences she had no idea of the effort that was going on behind the scenes, or of the adventure that was in store.

Nina's Story
Chapter Four

The Move to Mkomazi

At last the big day arrived. Nina was standing quietly in her enclosure when the Born Free team entered. They carried out a few final health checks to make sure she was fit to travel. Bandi told them how she liked to be talked to in a low, soft voice, how she was fond of stretching out her trunk . . . oh, and how she liked cake!

He explained how he often smuggled Nina treats from the kitchen, and how she'd scoop them out of his hand with her trunk with which she used to place each delicious morsel into her mouth. There was just one problem. Cake was not an ideal snack for an elephant, especially one who was about to make a return to the wild!

FACT FILE

An elephant's vegetarian diet consists of leaves, grasses, twigs and bark. They need a lot of vegetation to sustain their great size – up to 169kg a day! That's about the weight of two average, full-grown men or seven eight-year-old children. Elephants can spend up to sixteen hours a day finding food.

Unfortunately, Nina's love of cake, plus the lack of exercise space in her enclosure (and any reason to exercise), meant she was now overweight. This would hopefully change as soon as she was free and eating a wild elephant diet. Everyone was hoping Nina could be encouraged to walk happily into the transportation crate by herself.

Meanwhile, the TV crew discreetly set up their equipment, careful not to unsettle Nina with loud noises or too much chatter. Nina looked on while

Bandi stayed by her side, patting her reassuringly and stroking her trunk.

Hannibal maneuvered the massive transport crate into position, its open door filled the entrance to Nina's enclosure. Nina's carers, the people most familiar to her, tried cajoling her into the crate, calling her gently, and nudging her forward. She didn't move. She wasn't in the least bit interested. They tried luring her with bananas, but she backed away.

Eventually, Bandi Schwendt had an idea. He ran to the kitchen and came back with an entire delicious iced cake. He held out a piece of it with a flat hand. Nina glanced at the cake, stared at the crate, then lowered her eyelids and looked away.

'Come on girl, Nina, my temboli,'

Bandi crooned encouragingly.

He waved the tempting cake at the foot of the crate. If anything could entice Nina surely it would be her favourite treat. The crowd, including Will, Tony, Martin and the TV crew, held their breath and silently willed Nina to step forward. But Nina didn't budge.

Clem Coetzee had a plan. Clem had developed a way of giving just enough anaesthetic drug to sedate and calm an elephant, but not enough to make them sleep heavily. The team was keeping their fingers crossed that a large amount of anaesthetic wouldn't be needed anyway.

Clem prepared a dart that contained the anaesthetic. It needed to knock Nina out for just

enough time to allow the sixty-strong team to roll her onto the sliding floor of the crate and drag them, together, inside. With the door shut she would immediately be revived.

Talking to her in a calm, reassuring voice, Clem approached Nina and administered the drug. The team watched anxiously and waited for the drug to take effect. The seconds seem to pass so slowly. Clem said it would take up to eight minutes . . . then Nina stumbled forward, staggered and fell to the ground. Now, it was a question of moving her quickly and without causing her any harm.

Nina's body was quickly strapped with strong cables then, muscles bulging and sinews straining, the team dragged her onto the ramp and into the crate.

She was in a deep sleep so she wasn't aware of what was happening to her. The team had to make sure she wasn't in an awkward position and that she wasn't lying on her trunk, which could fatally restrict her breathing. Martin was given the job of stopping her trunk from twisting. Will and Tony also had to make sure that everyone involved was safe – especially as so many people were needed to position such a big animal.

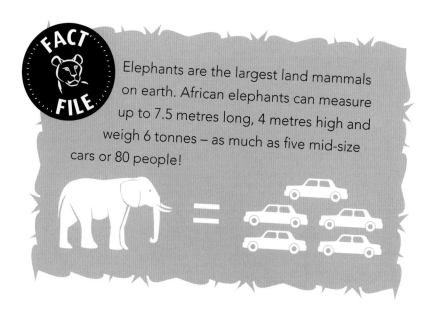

FACT FILE

Elephants are the largest land mammals on earth. African elephants can measure up to 7.5 metres long, 4 metres high and weigh 6 tonnes – as much as five mid-size cars or 80 people!

Once Nina was safely in place, the straps were removed. Still unconscious, she was given a thorough health check and the small puncture where she had been darted was treated with antibiotics, to prevent infection, and she was given an antidote to revive her. The door of the crate was closed. She came round with a blink and a flap of her ears.

The following morning, Hannibal and the rest of the convoy set off for the ten hour drive to Mkomazi. Clem made sure there were frequent stops along the way, just to make sure that Nina was all right and that

she had plenty of water. As the vehicles drove up the rust-coloured dirt road that led to the main camp, Nina remained blissfully unaware that she was now entering the terrain of her new home – hundreds of thousands of hectares of dry savannah and bush, surrounded by distant blue-hazed mountains.

The truck parked at the entrance to the special 'boma' compound that Tony had created. The crate was lowered gently to the ground so that the door opened into the enclosure. Nina was given her first glimpse of the world beyond Mount Meru. Film crews, dignitaries, Martin, Tony, Will, Bandi and the entire team hung from every ledge, hoping to catch the special moment.

Understandably, Nina was feeling a bit timid after her ordeal. She seemed reluctant to leave the 'safety' of the crate and step into her new world. They waited patiently. But they knew that Hannibal and the expert Kenya Wildlife Service operating team had to return urgently to Nairobi – a 20 hour drive. Eventually, Will took hold of Nina's tail and ever so gently encouraged her to step outside. She shuffled slowly to the middle. She stretched her trunk, found Martin's outstretched hand and, in it, a reassuring banana. She was fine.

Nina spent her next few days exploring the boma. It had been designed to give her lots of fun things to do, mimicking the natural environment of Mkomazi. There were large rocks and logs for her to rub her back against, cut branches for her to strip and eat and a plentiful supply of drinking water. The midday sun was fierce in this part of Tanzania, so at lunchtime she had to find shade beneath the special canopy Tony had installed. She also started throwing water over her back.

When it gets hot, elephants suck water into their trunks then blow it back out to shower themselves with a cool mist. They sometimes throw dust or mud over themselves to protect their skin from sunburn and biting insects. They also control their body temperature using their ears. The ears contain lots of little blood vessels, so by flapping them on a hot day, they increase the flow of air across the surface of the skin, which cools the blood and helps them stay comfortable.

Nina's Story
Chapter Five

Into the Wild

After a few days in the boma, Tony Fitzjohn observed that Nina seemed calm and settled enough to be released into the rest of the Park. This was the moment everyone had been waiting for. The TV crew gathered, cameras poised. The onlookers stood back.

The gates creaked wide. The path was clear. The endless bush beckoned. But Nina did nothing.

When elephants are relocated they are normally taken to a remote area with lots of natural food and water. Elephants – sometimes whole family groups – are regularly relocated in Kenya, especially when there have been clashes with local humans. It is

important that relocated elephants like their new environment, otherwise they may trek all the way back to where they came from.

The camera crew sighed and sat back. If not today, maybe tomorrow. The gates were left open and Nina skulked around the boma, eating, grazing and cooling herself. She searched hungrily for her favourite treat of bananas. Every day she guzzled bunches and bunches, hand fed to her by Tony – although cake was now off the menu!

Occasionally, Nina glanced at the open gate, but she never went near it, much to everyone's frustration. Perhaps she was so used to the small enclosure at Mount Meru that walls and fences felt reassuring to her. After all the effort, money and manpower it had taken to get her to Mkomazi, was this lovely but stubborn elephant choosing captivity over freedom?

The film crew left, disappointed that they hadn't witnessed the remarkable moment they had hoped for. Tony Fitzjohn decided the only way to lure Nina out of the boma was to make sure the outside world was a more tempting option. The obvious way to do

this was to ration her supply of bananas. If her favourite snack wasn't so plentiful, maybe she'd be tempted to look for it outside the boma.

For several days, Tony reduced the amount of bananas he fed her. Nina was not impressed. One day, she pushed him up against a wall and looked him in the eye, until he fed her another banana. She was clever and cheeky enough to realise that threatening to squash him was a way to get what she wanted. Tony knew she'd never really hurt him though.

Amazingly, for a further six weeks, Nina stayed in the boma. She ate, drank, rested, wallowed, covered herself in dust and rubbed her huge back against the rocks. Tony had almost given up hope of witnessing her great walk to freedom.

And then, one morning, without any fuss or fanfare, she ambled out of the gate. She stretched her trunk, gave a goodbye nudge to Tony and her astonished keepers, and was off.

Nina headed for one of the mountains, some six miles away, and there she spent the next two months admiring the landscape. Tony named the mountain Mlina Nina in her honour. It was one of the tallest mountains in the area, with wonderful views over the red plains and the snow-capped peak of Mount Kilimanjaro to the northwest.

After a few months, Nina went on the move. The Reserve rangers started spotting her in various locations around Mkomazi. Because it was so vast, Mkomazi offered plenty of terrain, from rocky hills and clusters of thornbush, to large stretches of rust-coloured earth studded with baobab trees.

Best of all, Nina had the company of other elephants. Maybe they were able to teach her about the Reserve's other inhabitants – the buffalo, lions, leopards, kudus, gazelles, aardwolves and the thousand or more species with which she would now share her life.

There was also plenty of edible vegetation in Mkomazi. Tony Fitzjohn and the Born Free team had been concerned that after being hand-fed in captivity, Nina would struggle to find food for herself.

They needn't have worried. She quickly learned survival skills, such as plucking fruit with her trunk or stripping branches of their leaves.

FACT FILE

An elephant's trunk is mainly used to prepare food and suck water. It can sense the size, shape and temperature of an object and can reach as high as 7 metres. An elephant's trunk can grow to be about 2 metres long and weigh up to 140 kg. It is made up of 150,000 muscles, but no bones and should an elephant decide to swim (and some do) it can be used like a snorkel under water!

As the years went by, Nina was spotted with several different groups of wild elephants. Despite being isolated for so long, she'd been accepted by her own kind. The loneliness she'd suffered in captivity, her

craving for the
company of other
elephants, was
now behind her.

Even so, every
few months, she
would wander
back to Tony's
camp to pay a visit to her human companions.
Tony and the team were always delighted to see her
and made sure they had a few bananas on hand
whenever she dropped by. They were also pleased to
see that her tusks had grown big and strong. She was
becoming the impressive, powerful elephant she was
born to be.

Tusks are an elephant's incisor teeth. They
are used for defence, digging for water
and roots and stripping bark off trees.
Tusks grow for most of an elephant's lifetime
and are an indicator of age. Elephants prefer one
tusk over the other, just as humans are either left or
right-handed.

FACT FILE

In November 2003, something magical happened. One morning, years later, Nina appeared in the grounds of Tony's camp. She strolled up to the workshop where he and his children were busy fixing fence-posts for the wild dog sanctuary and gave a friendly trumpet. They ran to greet her and immediately noticed she was looking rather fatter than she had in previous years.

And then, early the next morning, the reason for her size became clear. She caught the attention of one of the rangers, by prodding her trunk through his bedroom window. He came out and saw she had a new-born calf between her legs. Nina the extraordinary elephant had had a baby boy!

Tony and his team were overwhelmed with happiness – and thrilled that Nina felt so safe in their company that she had wanted to have her baby near them. Tony contacted Will and the Born Free team and they all decided to name the calf Jonny Wilkinson, after the rugby player who helped the England team win the Rugby World Cup that very afternoon.

Nina and Jonny didn't stay in the camp for long. They wandered off into the bush, destined to be together for several years, roaming, feeding and playing. Nina would have to teach him everything he needed to know about elephant habits and survival. Despite being a late starter, everyone was confident she would do a brilliant job.

Nina's Story
Chapter Six

A Sad Ending and a Happy One

Sure enough, Jonny Wilkinson thrived. He grew strong and healthy and over the next few years, together with Nina, he was often spotted around Mkomazi. Sometimes they were alone, and sometimes they were accompanied by five males. When Nina had first arrived at Mkomazi, there had been several elephant experts who had said that it was unlikely she'd mate and have a calf, as a result of being isolated from other elephants for so long. Once again, Nina had proved everyone wrong.

FACT
FILE

By the time most elephants reach 13 years old, they are mature enough to have their first calf. Elephants have the longest pregnancy of all mammals, taking 22 months from conception to birth. Elephants are very attentive mothers, and because most elephant behaviour has to be learned, they keep their offspring with them for many years.

After four years, Nina and Jonny Wilkinson came to visit Tony's camp once again. As usual, they had several large bull elephants with them. At first, Tony was delighted to see that mother and son were still together, but then he observed that Nina seemed keen to hand Jonny Wilkinson over to the care of one of the bulls.

As Nina made her way towards Tony, he sensed something wasn't right. She was looking fat again, but limping slightly and she didn't seem quite herself. Tony gave her a cuddle and a pat. He even offered her a banana, but she refused. Instead she stretched out her trunk and gave a tired blink.

Worried about his favourite elephant, Tony decided to keep an eye on her. He was relieved when she chose to linger near the camp. But at the same time, he could see that the bull elephant companions were also unusually attentive. If she called for their help they'd come. Tony didn't want to interfere with their natural bond.

FACT FILE

Elephants make low-frequency calls, many of which, though incredibly loud, are too low for humans to hear. These sounds allow elephants to communicate with one another over distances of up to 2.5 km. Elephants can also use their feet to listen, by picking up sub-sonic rumblings made by other elephants, through vibrations in the ground. In this way they are able to 'hear' the noises made by other elephants up to 10km away.

A day later, something terrible happened. Tony noticed a sour smell in the air and tracked it to an area of scrub, less than a kilometre from the boma where Nina had first been released. There, he found her, lying on her side, buzzing with flies. He could tell immediately that she was dead.

Tony was devastated. He quickly recruited one of his rangers and together they performed an autopsy on Nina's body. It was important to find out how she had died, so that they might be able to help future elephants. They soon discovered that Nina had been pregnant again. Her calf had been facing the wrong way and had become stuck during delivery. This had put great stress on her body and caused her death.

Tony knew there was nothing they could have done for her or her calf. Every year, healthy wild elephants die in the same circumstances. It was terribly sad but at least it was a natural death. Even so, Nina was more to Tony, Martin, Will and Bandi than just a wild elephant – she was a friend and they had been on an incredible journey together.

Tony was sorry he hadn't been with Nina in her final hours, but grateful that her elephant companions had brought her back to him, as though they knew it was where she wanted to be.

That evening, he walked down to a nearby airstrip to watch the sunset. Suddenly, a herd of thirty elephants emerged from the bush and silently crossed the Tana River in front of him. Tony had no idea where these majestic elephants were heading or what they were going to do, but in that moment, he knew that, together with Bandi Schwendt Nagy, Will Travers and the Born Free team, Martin Clunes and Clem Coetzee, they had done the right thing for Nina. She'd died at a fairly young age, but thanks to their efforts, she'd been given many years of freedom. She'd had the chance, against all odds, to be a wild elephant.

The sad ending to Nina's story must not take away all the positives that it has brought. She is proof that even after 27 years in captivity, elephants can be returned successfully to the wild. Not only can they survive, but they can thrive and make friends with wild elephants and re-join elephant society.

The fact that Nina conceived, delivered and weaned a healthy calf is also an incredible achievement. Jonny Wilkinson continues to do well and since Nina's death, he has been spotted with a bachelor group of young bull elephants. When he matures and becomes a prime bull he may well go onto mate and have young of his own. Mating is vital if endangered

elephant populations are to grow again – especially when the threats from ivory poaching are on the increase.

Elephants have
no natural predator,
although lions will
sometimes prey
on young or weak
elephants in the wild.
The main risk to

elephants is from humans, through poaching and the
conversion of wild habitat into farmland. Every year,
tens of thousands of elephants are killed for their
ivory tusks.

Thanks to Nina's starring role in the 'Born to be
Wild' BBC documentary, awareness of the plight
of Africa's wildlife has increased. The programme
was aired on New Year's Day 1998, to an audience of
thirteen million. Nina's story was a hit and the life-
saving work of the Born Free Foundation was given
a massive boost. The popularity of the documentary
meant they received more support, raised more
money, and ultimately, helped more animals.

Despite the challenges involved in Nina's rescue,
Born Free and an amazing team of dedicated
individuals, proved it could be done and, most

importantly, they made a huge difference to Nina's quality of life. She may have been only one elephant, but Born Free believes that individuals matter.

No doubt Nina, herself, would agree.

Pinkie's Story
Chapter Seven

Far away from the dry plains of Africa, deep in the lowland dry zone of Sri Lanka, another baby elephant faced a trauma.

FACT FILE

Elephants are found in Africa and Asia. There are two African species and one Asian. Elephants are highly adaptable creatures. They can cope with many different environments, ranging from the forests and plains of Asia to the savannahs and tropical jungles of Africa, as long as there is enough space, food and water. Male and female African elephants (whose ears are shaped like Africa) have tusks. Asian elephants' ears are shaped like India and only males have tusks.

The little elephant in this story was only three months old when she fell into a disused quarry. The quarry was flooded with water. She had been trying to drink from it, but had lost her footing and toppled in.

After struggling to get out for a few minutes, she began screeching in fright. Her mother stood at the edge, reaching down with her trunk, trumpeting back to her baby, but there was nothing she could do. The pit was too deep.

As the calf continued to struggle she received many scratches and bruises. The walls were rocky and jagged. Every time she managed to climb a little way out, she slipped back. The longer this went on, the more distressed she became – so, too, did her mother. Being separated from her baby and unable to help her must have been devastating.

Days went by. The little elephant wore her toenails away through her constant scrabbling up the rough walls. She also gashed her cheek, just below her right eye, causing her to bleed heavily. To make matters worse, she couldn't get milk from her mother. She started to grow weaker.

The situation looked hopeless. But just then, out of the thick maze of rainforest shrub, a local villager called Weerasinghe appeared. He'd been walking with his dog, minding his own business, when he stumbled across this troubling scene.

At first Weerasinghe was nervous. People and wild elephants don't usually get along. He remembered all the stories from his village, of angry elephants trampling homes and eating crops. He caught sight

of the calf's mother, lurking in the nearby trees. She was as large as any elephant he'd seen. If she charged at him, she would kill him. She spread her ears and gave a loud trumpet.

FACT FILE

Sometimes elephants communicate with an ear-splitting blast when in danger or alarmed, causing others to form a protective circle around the younger members of the family group. They also use their ears to signal or warn other elephants that they are angry, by bringing them forward and fully extending them.

Weerasinghe wanted to flee, but when he looked down at the baby in the hole, he was heartbroken by her delicate, sorrowful face. She looked so scared and vulnerable.

In a split second, he decided to do what he could to help her. He jumped into the hole and began to haul her out. Although she was much smaller than a full-grown elephant, she still weighed about 91 kg and stood at 1 metre high – that's 25 times the size of the average human baby!

Somehow, Weerasinghe – a slim man using his bare hands – found the strength he needed to free the young calf. He pushed her up and out of the hole. Exhausted, he climbed out, stood back and caught his breath. The dazed calf stared at her saviour, then at his dog. She'd probably never seen a dog before, let alone a human.

But there was no time for Weerasinghe to congratulate himself or make friends. He sensed that the baby's mother was looking at him and feeling nervous of what she might do next, he finally ran away.

It wasn't until he got back to his village, to the familiar site of the wooden huts, roaming chickens and the smell of the cooking fires, that he felt safe. But all of a sudden, he realised he'd left without his dog. Not to worry, he thought. His dog was a clever animal. He'd find his way home. Weerasinghe set to work around the yard. He waved to a neighbour and fed his prize pig. He forgot about the baby elephant he'd rescued.

An hour or so later, the dog returned. Weerasinghe was pleased to see him – and then shocked to see that his canine companion was not alone. Right behind him was the baby elephant! Weerasinghe blinked and gasped. This couldn't be! An elephant in a village – even a baby – could only mean trouble.

The elephant gave a tiny, hopeful cry. Why had she followed the dog and not gone with her elephant mother instead? Had the ordeal confused her? Weerasinghe scratched his head. He wanted to shoo the baby away, but once again, he couldn't help but taking pity on her.

It wasn't long before word spread through the village. Soon, the little elephant had quite an audience. The children thought she was wonderful, but the adults were alarmed. They were worried the baby's mother would come looking for her, that she would damage their village, or worse, try to hurt them.

Weerasinghe decided to take advice from the head priest at his local Buddhist temple. The priest was wise and kind and knew what to do. He reassured the villagers that they needn't fear the little elephant. He also knew it was too late to try to reunite the calf with her mother. Having been unable to feed her for days,

86

her milk supply would have dried up. But without milk, the baby elephant wouldn't survive, so something needed to be done, and quickly.

The priest handed Weerasinghe a phone and told him to call the Elephant Transit Home (ETH), a rescue, rehabilitation and release facility for elephants, run by Sri Lanka's Department of Wildlife Conservation and supported by the Born Free Foundation. Staff at the ETH wasted no time. The next day, a young vet called Dr Suhada Jayewardene arrived with a team of people. They collected the baby and took her back to the ETH headquarters. Once the elephant was settled, the team knew their first priority was to make sure she was fed. Dr Suhada was worried that their regular milk formula would be too rich for the calf's fragile digestion. He decided to give her a special milk solution that was lighter and gentler than usual. She was fed through a funnel with a tube that went into her mouth.

The next priority was to see to her injuries, which, if left untreated, could lead to life threatening infections. Dr Suhada gave her some antibiotics and

applied a healing ointment called gentian violet to her wounds. The ointment was pink in colour, which he liberally applied to the long, pink wound under her right eye.

The next day, Dr Suhada began to treat the worst wounds more thoroughly. He was very worried about the gash under Pinkie's eye. It was starting to turn septic and he had to get it under control before it claimed her life. He removed the bad skin tissue and applied more antibiotics. Then it was a matter of waiting and watching.

Luckily, after a week, Pinkie started to recover. The team began feeding her standard milk formula and she gained strength. After a few months she was fit enough to join the ETH's other young elephants in a large open paddock area. She soon found her confidence and became a gregarious and friendly member of the herd. They were all orphans like her, who, had they not been rescued by the ETH, would have faced a slow, painful death.

Several years later, aged about four, Pinkie and nine of her orphan friends were returned to Udawalawe National Park. In the past, rescued elephant orphans would have been trained, tamed and forced into a life of captivity, as working or ceremonial animals. Now, thanks to the ETH's intervention and Born Free's support, these orphans were given the chance to return to their natural habitat and have a free life.

The exciting moment of Pinkie's release was attended by members of the Sri Lankan government, as well as a group of Buddhist monks who blessed the animals. Pinkie was the last orphan to be loaded onto the truck. She walked confidently onto the vehicle without needing any encouragement. An hour later the truck arrived at the release sight in the middle of the park. She might have been the last on, but Pinkie was one of the first out, raising her trunk and trumpeting loudly. She was leading her friends to freedom.

The group of elephants stayed near the trucks for a short while, and then moved off into the forest. They have been monitored since and seem to be enjoying their new wild existence. As a group they like to stick together, but Pinkie is always distinguishable, due to the vivid pink scar from the healed wound below her right eye. Her scar is a reminder of her traumatic ordeal, but it is also a symbol of hope. When this little orphaned elephant was given the chance of life, she grabbed it with all her might.

Read all the rescue stories

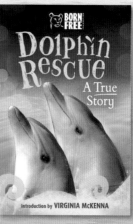

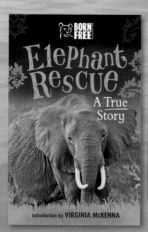

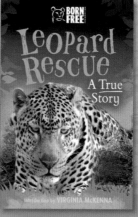

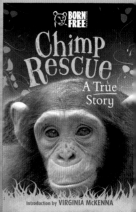

Keep Wildlife in the Wild

Go wild with Born Free

Welcome to the Born Free Foundation, where people get into animals and go wild! Our wildlife charity takes action all around the world to save lions, elephants, gorillas, tigers, chimps, dolphins, bears, wolves and lots more.

If you're wild about animals visit
www.bornfree.org.uk
to find out more, join our free kids' club WildcreW or adopt your own animal.

Keep Wildlife in the Wild

We would like to extend a big thank you to the following people and organisations that made these incredible rescues possible. Their resolve and support were truly invaluable and for that we and the animals will be forever grateful.

Nina:

Martin Clunes

Clem Coetzee
(deceased)

Tony Fitzjohn

Lucy Fitzjohn

KWS and the KWS
Capture Team

Bandi Schwendt Nagy

The Tanzanian
Wildlife Authorities

The BBC –
Michael Massey

Andreas Bifani

The Born Free team

Pinkie:

Weerasinghe

Dr Suhada Jayewardene
and the team at the
Elephant Transit Home

Staff at the Department
of Wildlife Conservation,
Sri Lanka

The Born Free team